**Our Values**

# RESPECTING RULES & LAWS

By Steffi Cavell-Clarke

**Published in Canada**
Crabtree Publishing
616 Welland Avenue
St. Catharines, ON
L2M 5V6

**Published in the United States**
Crabtree Publishing
PMB 59051
350 Fifth Ave, 59th Floor
New York, NY 10118

**Published by Crabtree Publishing Company in 2019**

©2018 BookLife Publishing

**Author:** Steffi Cavell-Clarke

**Editors:** Kirsty Holmes, Janine Deschenes

**Design:** Jasmine Pointer

**Proofreader:** Melissa Boyce

**Production coordinator and
prepress technician (interior):** Margaret Amy Salter

**Prepress technician (covers):** Ken Wright

**Print coordinator:** Katherine Berti

**Photographs**

**Shutterstock:** ©kenny1 cover

All images from Shutterstock

Printed in the U.S.A./122018/CG20181005

**Library and Archives Canada Cataloguing in Publication**

Cavell-Clarke, Steffi, author
        Respecting rules and laws / Steffi Cavell-Clarke.

(Our values)
Includes index.
Issued in print and electronic formats.
ISBN 978-0-7787-5427-5 (hardcover).--
ISBN 978-0-7787-5494-7 (softcover).--ISBN 978-1-4271-2222-3 (HTML)

        1. Law--Juvenile literature.  2. Rule of law--Juvenile literature.
I. Title.

K250.C38 2018          j340'.11          C2018-905493-X
                                          C2018-905494-8

**Library of Congress Cataloging-in-Publication Data**

Names: Cavell-Clarke, Steffi, author.
Title: Respecting rules and laws / Steffi Cavell-Clarke.
Description: New York, New York : Crabtree Publishing Company, [2018] |
  Series: Our values | Includes index.
Identifiers: LCCN 2018043789 (print) | LCCN 2018044228 (ebook) |
  ISBN 9781427122223 (Electronic) |
  ISBN 9780778754275 (hardcover) |
  ISBN 9780778754947 (pbk.)
Subjects: LCSH: Law--Juvenile literature. | Rule of law--Juvenile literature.
Classification: LCC K250 (ebook) | LCC K250 .C39 2018 (print) |
  DDC 340/.11--dc23
LC record available at https://lccn.loc.gov/2018043789

# CONTENTS

Words that look like **this** can be found in the glossary on page 24.

# WHAT ARE VALUES?

Values are ideas and beliefs that we feel are important. Sharing values with others helps us to work and live together peacefully in a **community**. Values teach us how to **respect** each other and ourselves.

Spending money responsibly

Making positive choices

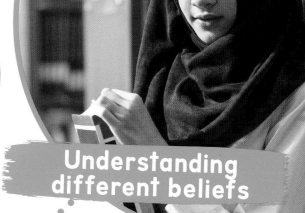
Understanding different beliefs

Values make our communities better places to live. Think about the values in your community. What is important to you and the people around you?

Respecting the law

Helping others

Listening to others

5

# WHAT ARE RULES?

Rules are **guidelines** that tell us what we should and should not do. They are created by responsible adults, such as parents or teachers. Rules tell you how to behave in different places. Your school, home, and community center are all places that have rules.

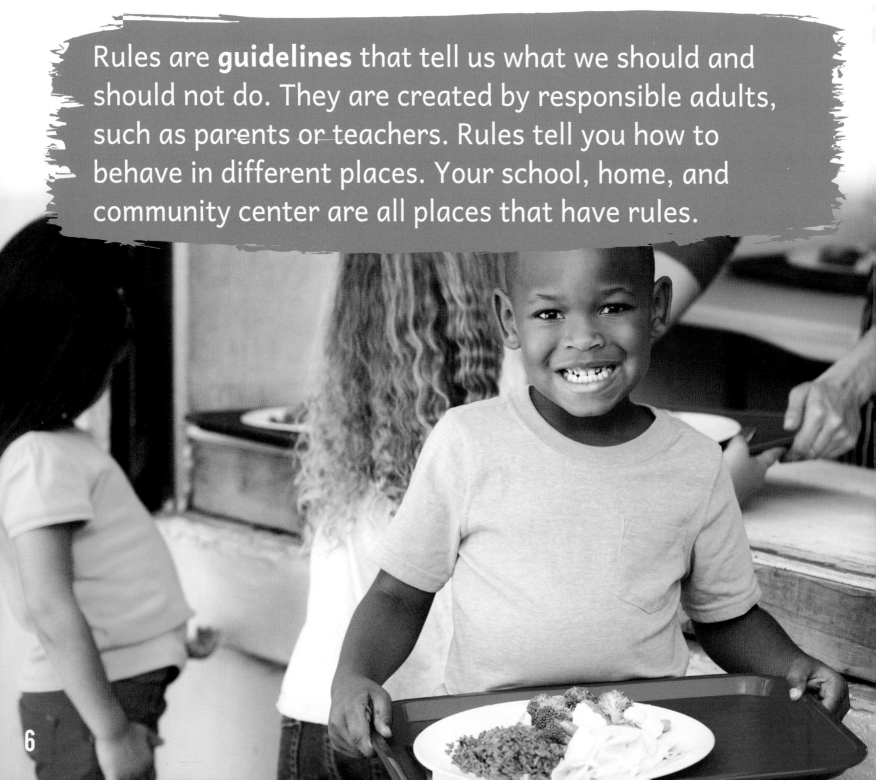

Rules are often created to keep people safe. A rule that we must wear a helmet when riding a bicycle keeps us safe. Many other rules make sure that people in a place respect each other.

A rule about staying silent in the library makes sure that other people are not disturbed while they read or work.

# WHY DO WE NEED RULES?

Rules help us to understand what is right and wrong. They guide our actions and help us make the right choices. They also help children and adults stay safe.

Following rules can also prepare us to follow laws. Find out more about laws on page 12.

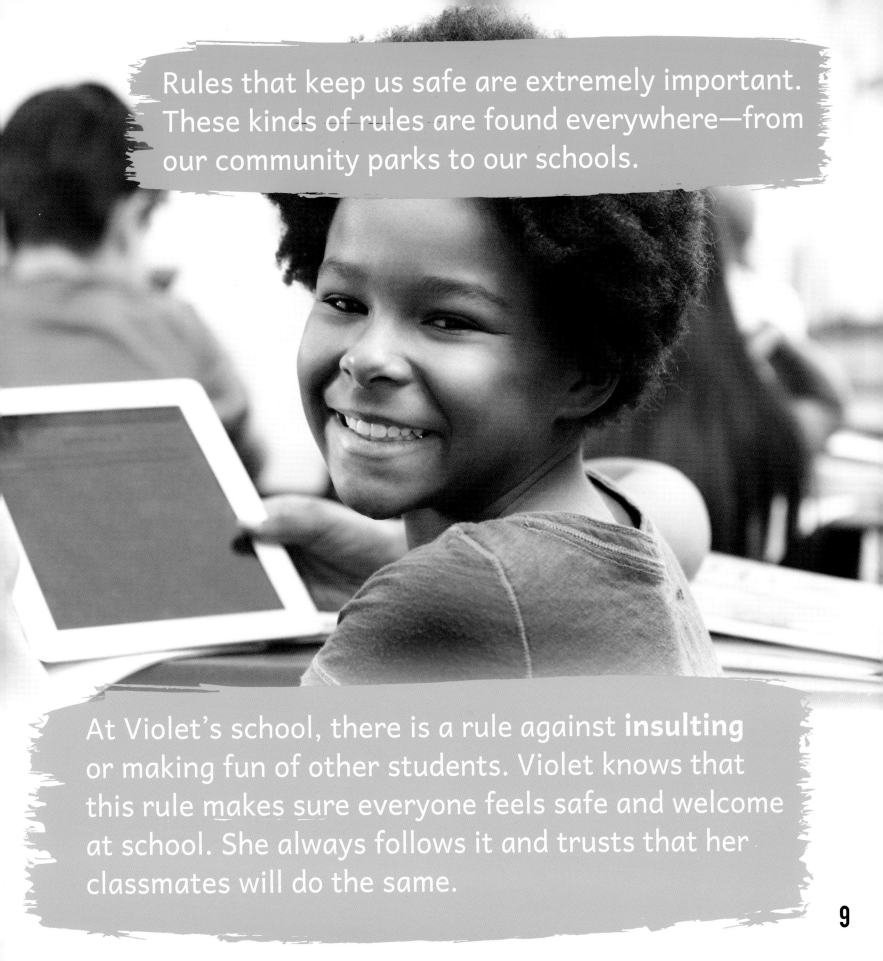

Rules that keep us safe are extremely important. These kinds of rules are found everywhere—from our community parks to our schools.

At Violet's school, there is a rule against **insulting** or making fun of other students. Violet knows that this rule makes sure everyone feels safe and welcome at school. She always follows it and trusts that her classmates will do the same.

# MAKING CHOICES

We all have choices when it comes to rules. We can choose to follow them and do our part to make sure everyone is safe and respected. We can also choose not to follow rules. This choice often leads to **consequences**.

Dylan threw his football inside the house, even though he knew it was against the rules. Now he isn't allowed to play with the ball for the rest of the week.

There may be a time when you do not agree with a rule, or the rules make you feel unsafe. You should always talk to a responsible and trusted adult to help you understand the rules, and the consequences of breaking them.

# WHAT ARE LAWS?

Laws are rules that everyone in a community, a state or province, or a country must follow. They are set up by **governments**. Laws help people to live, work, and play fairly and safely in their communities.

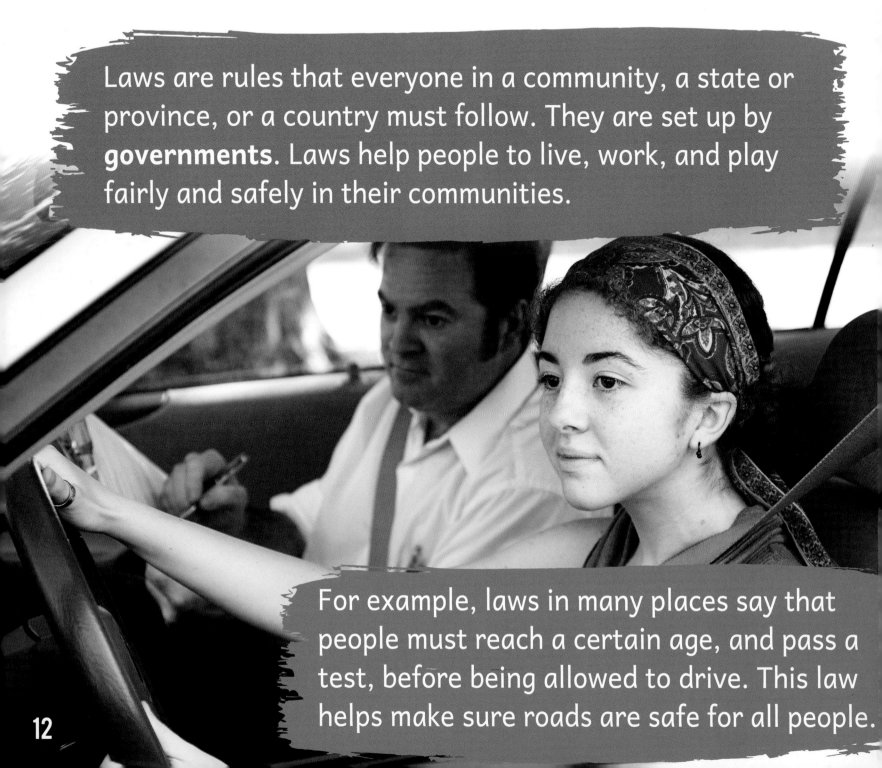

For example, laws in many places say that people must reach a certain age, and pass a test, before being allowed to drive. This law helps make sure roads are safe for all people.

Laws include things like not stealing, or not harming other people. Laws might also say at what age people are allowed to do things, such as marry or **vote**. These laws are meant to make sure people are old enough to understand the consequences of big decisions before they make them.

POLLING PLACE HERE
VOTACION
AQUI

POLLING
PLACE

# WHY ARE LAWS HELPFUL?

Laws are in place to make sure that everyone obeys the same rules. For people to be treated fairly in a community, everyone must be held to the same standard of behavior. Laws tell people how they should behave. They help people make the right choices. They also help keep everyone safe.

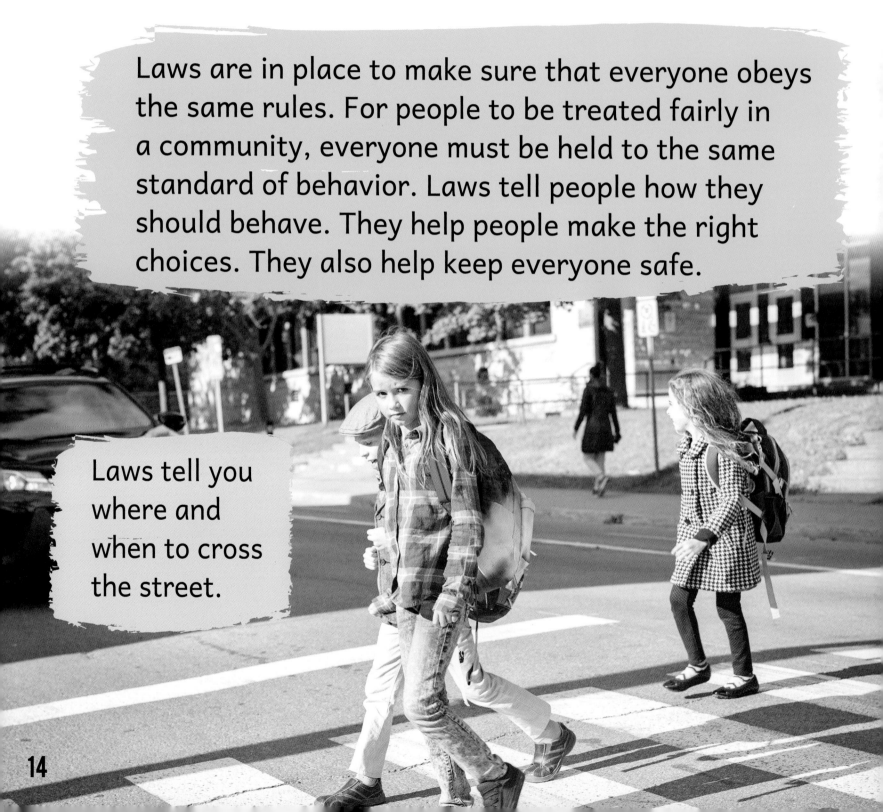

Laws tell you where and when to cross the street.

Think about the laws in place in your community. How do they work to keep all of the members of your community safe? How do they make sure that everyone is treated fairly and with respect?

# FACING CONSEQUENCES

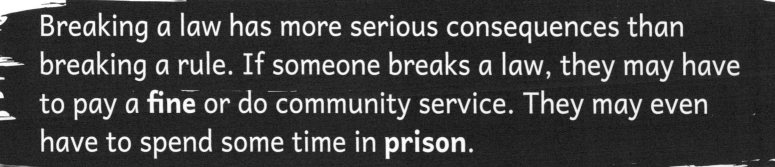

Breaking a law has more serious consequences than breaking a rule. If someone breaks a law, they may have to pay a **fine** or do community service. They may even have to spend some time in **prison**.

Community service is sometimes a punishment for breaking the law. It means a person must spend a certain amount of time doing something that benefits their community, such as cleaning up garbage.

Police officers are people who help everyone in the community. They have a very important job to do. They make sure that people follow the law, and they try to keep us safe from harm.

Police officers are people you can trust to keep your community safe.

# RESPECTING RULES AT SCHOOL

Every school has a set of rules that students must follow. Following rules at school helps it be a positive and safe place to learn. Rules help teachers do their jobs. They make sure that students are ready and able to learn.

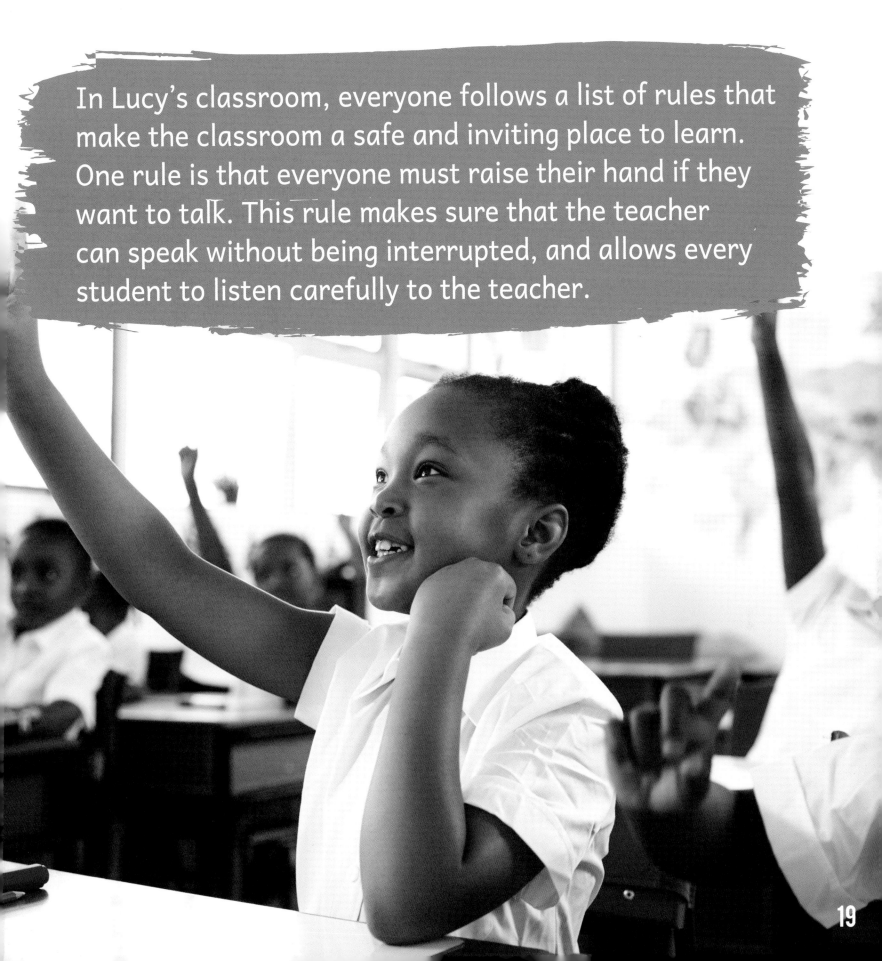

In Lucy's classroom, everyone follows a list of rules that make the classroom a safe and inviting place to learn. One rule is that everyone must raise their hand if they want to talk. This rule makes sure that the teacher can speak without being interrupted, and allows every student to listen carefully to the teacher.

# RESPECTING RULES AT HOME

We often have rules at home that allow everyone to live together happily. Rules can also encourage us to help each other.

William must help his parents clean the table and put away dishes after dinner. Doing jobs like these together means that William and his family will have more time to play games later.

Different families have different rules. One family might have rules about looking after their pets, while other families may have a rule that doesn't allow animals in the house.

# THE GOLDEN RULE

Following rules helps you stay safe and make the right choices. Remember that the most important rule to follow is to treat others the way you would like to be treated. This is called the Golden Rule.

You should never break the Golden Rule, even if other people **pressure** you to do so. You should also refuse if someone tries to convince you to break any other rule. It is important to talk to a responsible and trusted adult if this happens.

# GLOSSARY

**community** [kuh-MYOO-ni-tee] A group of people who live, work, and play in a place

**consequences** [KON-si-kwens-es] Results or outcomes of an action or choice

**fine** [fahyn] Money paid as a punishment or consequence

**governments** [GUHV-ern-muhnts] A group of people that govern, or control, a country, state or province, city, or other community

**guidelines** [GAHYD-layhns] Information that guides, or tells, people how they should behave or how something should be done

**insulting** [in-SUHL-ting] Making disrespectful or hurtful comments toward someone

**law** [law] Rule made by government that people must follow

**pressure** [PRESH-er] Trying to convince or persuade

**prison** [PRIZ-uhn] A place in which people are held in punishment for a crime

**respect** [ri-SPEKT] Give someone or something the care or attention it deserves

**responsibly** [ri-SPON-suh-blee] Doing something in a dependable and trustworthy way

**vote** [voht] Choose who will be part of government

# INDEX